PREISNEI

GW00659451

10 EASY PIECES FOR PIANO
10 ŁATWYCH UTWORÓW NA FORTEPIAN

INTERPRETED BY
LESZEK MOŻDŻER

Transcribed by Jack Long

Chester Music

This score has been transcribed as accurately as possible from the CD performance, but minor differences will exist.

Exclusive distributors:
Hal Leonard Europe Limited
42 Wigmore Street Marylebone, London, W1U 2RY
Email: info@halleonardeurope.com

This book © Copyright 2000 Chester Music.
Order No. CH61655 ISBN 0-7119-7885-9

Design by Chloë Alexander
Music setting by Enigma Music Production Services

CONTENTS

PREISNER'S
10 Easy Pieces for Piano

Only a few hours after the final notes of the world premiere of *Requiem for my friend*, his majestic piece for soloists, choir and orchestra, had died away in Warsaw's Grand Theatre in the autumn of 1998, Zbigniew Preisner was already looking ahead. The *Requiem*, dedicated to the late film director Krzysztof Kieslowski, had provided an ambitious and highly affecting summary of an important phase in Preisner's career, during which he had composed the music for Kieslowski's *Dekalog* sequence, *The Double Life of Veronika*, and the *Colours* trilogy. The two of them, together with the scenarist Krzysztof Piesiewicz, had created a wonderfully collaborative form of cinema, in which images, ideas, words and music combined to touch the emotions of audiences around the world. Now, having mourned the loss of a close friend and artistic inspiration, it was time to move on.

"When people like Krzysztof die," Preisner said that day in Warsaw, "the question to be answered is whether those of us who are left have enough strength to take over from them. Whether we have enough strength to say, 'Now it's our time. Now look at us.' Do we have enough talent? Until we try, we don't know. We know that there is a future waiting for us. Some of us are involved in the thing called art – I don't like the word, but I don't know a better one. We were born from the art, and were educated by it. And we have a duty to do something more. Somebody has left us something, and we too must leave something, some testimony of our time."

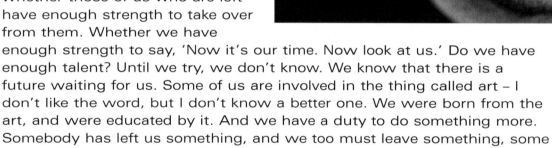

In *10 Easy Pieces for Piano* we find the first installment of Preisner's post-Kieslowski testimony. And, in a sense, it could hardly be further away from the most obvious qualities of the music for which the composer became famous. Whereas the soundtracks and the *Requiem* were noted for the ravishing beauty of their orchestrations, in which unusual instrumental combinations were often deployed around the voice of the soprano Elzbieta Towarnicka, these piano pieces focus on an economy of means.

Yet no listener will be in any doubt about the identity of the composer. Preisner's highly personal sense of lyricism sings as clearly as ever throughout these pieces, creating a music formed by one man's soul yet existing beyond boundaries of geography or style, speaking to listeners unwilling to limit their responses according to pre-existing definitions of taste.

The briefest outline of Preisner's career perhaps offers some explanation for an inherent resistance to frontiers and limitations. Brought up in a small Polish village, he was the son of a chemical engineer who played the accordion at weddings and birthday parties. He grew up, therefore, with music as an everyday thing, part of the vernacular of life. Later he studied art history at the university in Karkow before joining a cabaret for which he wrote songs and played the piano. Meanwhile, he taught himself music theory and compositional technique from textbooks. "It's more important who you're with and what you're inspired by. I'm not inspired by music. I'm interested in literature, philosophy, life, painting, people. I happened to grow up with folk music, which is something to remember and to get something from. But when you're composing music, you never know where it comes from."

The inspiration for *10 Easy Pieces for Piano* came out of his own reaction to the success of the *Requiem*. "I like contrast very much," he said. "And after making music of such monumental scale, I wanted to do something simple. I also like the piano. And it seemed to me that one form of music which could be both simple and complex was music for solo piano. I like very much all the music recorded by Keith Jarrett, particularly the famous *Köln Concert*. Listening to that for the first time, many years ago, was a great experience for me. Maybe it inspired me to do something similar."

Another inspiration, he said, was his friendship with the pianist Leszek Możdżer, a product of the Gdansk music school, who has given classical recitals, played with the great Polish jazz musicians Tomasz Stanko and Zbigniew Namyslowski, and recorded his own remarkable interpretations of Chopin's piano pieces. "I believe that he is a very great talent," Preisner remarked. "I've known him for many years. We first worked together on the soundtrack for the Louis Malle film, *Damage*, and later on the music for *People's Century*, the BBC TV's documentary series. But all the time I felt that when I gave him the notes I was limiting him in some way, not allowing him to show everything he could do. So for this record I wanted to give him such an opportunity, to give him more room for interpretation, which wouldn't

have been so easy if it had been written for piano and orchestra. It's hard to explain in general terms how much scope for interpretation he had, because each of the pieces has its own logic. The only piece where it's obvious is the one called *Talking to Myself*. In that one, you can tell quite easily where is the theme and where is his improvisation. But in all these pieces, it was an enormous experience for me to listen to the music being born from the notes I gave him."

If this music limits its resource to a single instrument, that is not to suggest that it is shorn of textural variety. Inspired by the lyricism and dynamic range of Preisner's writing, Leszek Możdżer draws from the piano a range of timbres and sonorities exploiting all the instrument's physical properties – its wood and wire, its cavities and reflecting surfaces – as he follows a sequence that moves from limpid reveries to full-throttle aggression and back again.

Many people first became acquainted with Preisner through the heartbreaking *Concerto in E minor*, which the script of *The Double Life of Veronika* presented as the work of a fictional composer, one Van Den Budenmayer. That music, we came to learn, was in fact full-strength Preisner. And so, in a different guise, are these *10 Easy Pieces for Piano*, a new and fascinating part of the evolving testimony of one of the most remarkable composers of our time.

Richard Williams

LESZEK MOŻDŻER

Leszek Możdżer (pronounced Leshek Mozhder) is one of the greatest keyboard talents in the Polish music scene today.

Born in 1971, Możdżer has been playing the piano since he was five. He graduated from the Stanislaw Moniuszko Conservatory in Gdansk in 1996, having developed his interest in jazz at the age of 18 at high school. He started his jazz career by joining the band of clarinet player Emil Kowalski, but he considers that his true development began with the Milosc Band in 1991. A year later, he received an individual citation from the Jazz Junior '92 International Competition in Krakow, followed immediately by many other prizes including the Krzysztof Komeda Prize 1992 from the Polish Culture Foundation; the First Prize of the International Jazz Improvisation Competition in Katowice in 1994; the Mateusz Swiecicki Prize from Polish Radio 3; the Mayor of Gdansk's medal for outstanding artistic achievements; the Fryderyk Prize for Jazz Musician of 1998; as well as many citations in the magazine Jazz Forum, including being nominated six times as Best Pianist between 1993 and 1998.

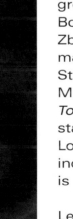

During the six years in which Możdżer led Milosc, it became the most popular jazz group in Poland. He recorded six albums with the group, including two with the American trumpeter, Lester Bowie. At the same time, he was a star attraction of the Zbigniew Namyslowski Quartet. Możdżer has performed with many outstanding Polish jazz musicians, including Tomasz Stanko (*Farewell to Mary*), Janusz Muniak (*One and Four*), Michael Urbaniak (*Live in Holy City*), and Piotr Wojtasik (*Lonely Town*, *Quest*). He has also collaborated with such international stars as Arthur Blythe, Buster Williams, Billy Harper, Joe Lovano and Archie Shepp. Możdżer has recorded 30 CDs, including four under his own name, the best known of which is *Chopin Impressions*.

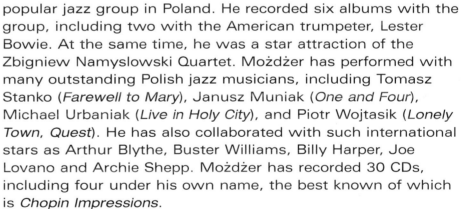

Leszek Możdżer has given concerts in Italy, Germany, Spain, Switzerland, the Czech Republic, Slovakia, Greece, Denmark, Sweden, Finland, Russia, Kazakhstan, Kyrgystan, USA, Hungary and France. At the prestigious Piano Festival in La Chartes, his jazz interpretations of Chopin's pieces received a standing ovation.

Since 1992 Możdżer has been a regular collaborator with Zbigniew Preisner, taking part in the recording of many of the composer's film scores. *10 Easy Pieces for Piano* was specially written by Preisner for Możdżer.

A Good Morning Melody

Melodia na dzień dobry

I cannot sleep, so I go outside, and see an unearthly view:
below my house window, everything is floating in fog, just as if the
mansion was hanging somewhere in clouds and flying.
It's a pity it doesn't fly.
How good that I couldn't sleep.

Maszyce, 6 May 1998, about 5:30a.m.

Zbigniew Preisner
Interpreted by Leszek Możdżer

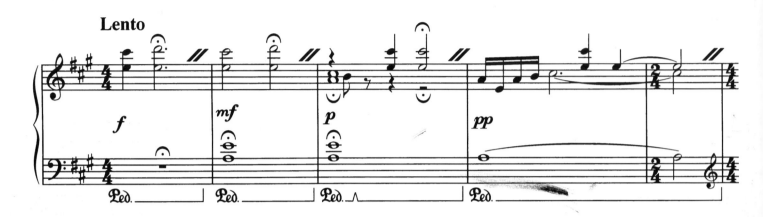

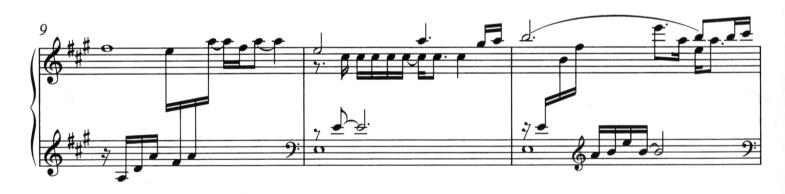

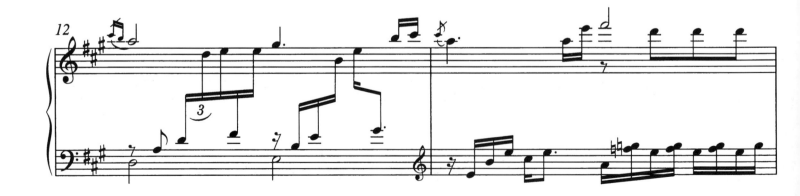

Meditation

Zaduma

7 July

Zbigniew Preisner
Interpreted by Leszek Możdżer

A new day is just like new life, or another page in an unfinished book.
Life is going on; what's on today?

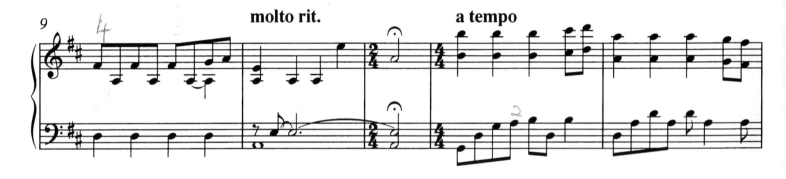

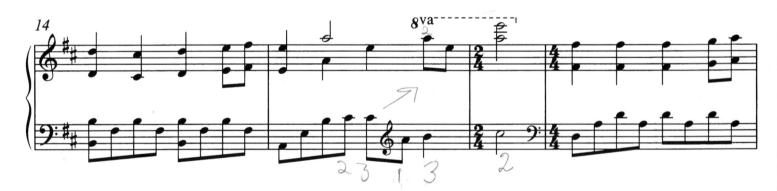

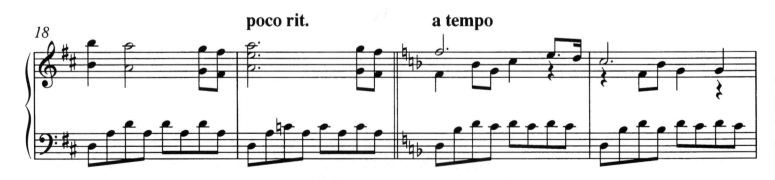

To See More

Widzieć więcej

13 July

sometimes, I feel like flying high beyond everything and against everybody. I wish I could do it today. Energy is necessary to live, 'the will of life is the will of struggle'.

Zbigniew Preisner
Interpreted by Leszek Możdżer

Ped. ad lib.

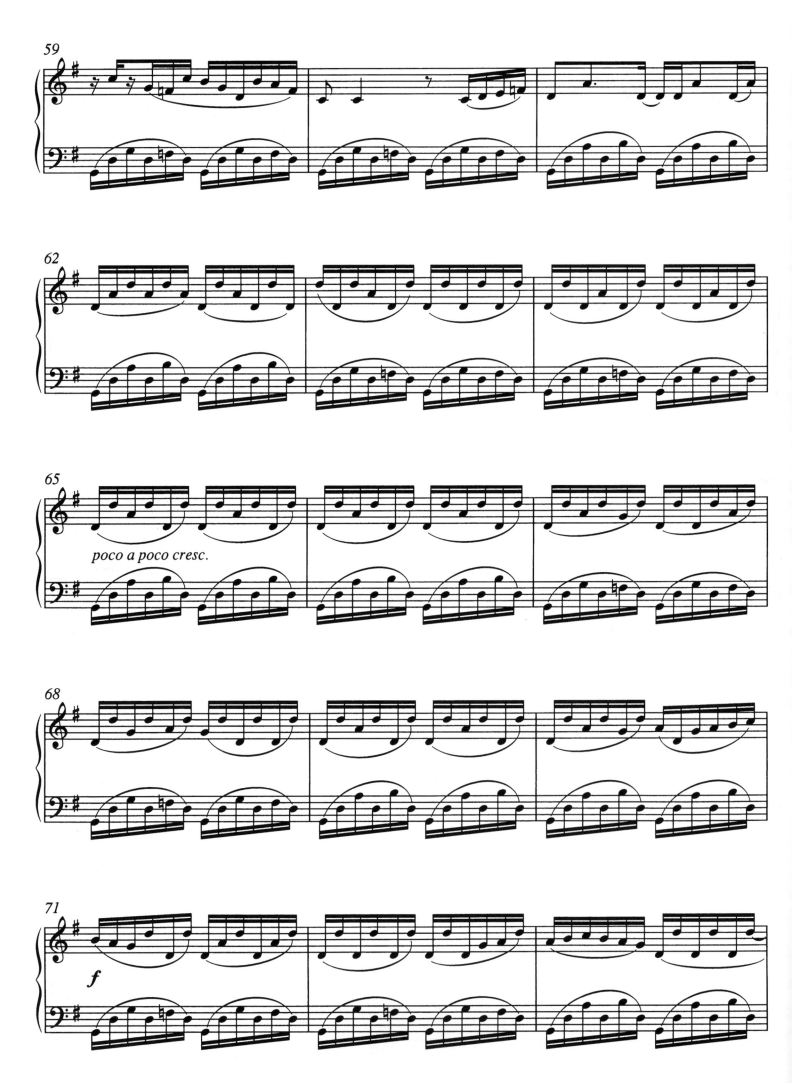

Talking To Myself

Rozmowa z samym soba

I like to return here because the silence of this place provokes me to contemplate. Nothing impedes my thinking, nothing roars me down and nobody's in a hurry. Delightful silence. i'm petrified.

'Leśny Dwór', Wetlina. 1 August

Zbigniew Preisner
Interpreted by Leszek Możdżer

Lento, ma liberamente

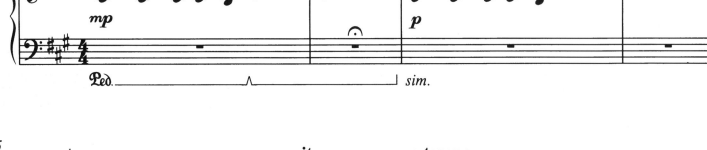

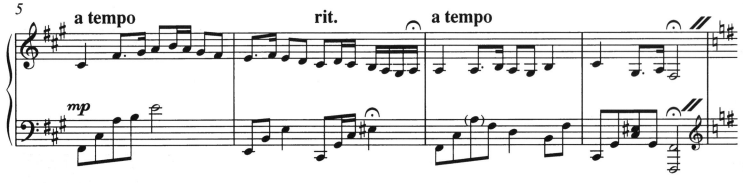

Presto
senza misura *without meter*

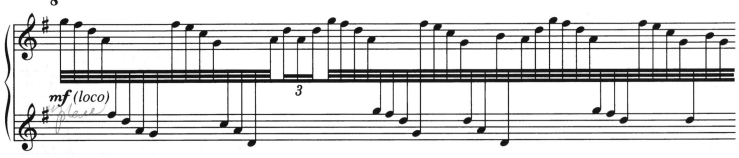

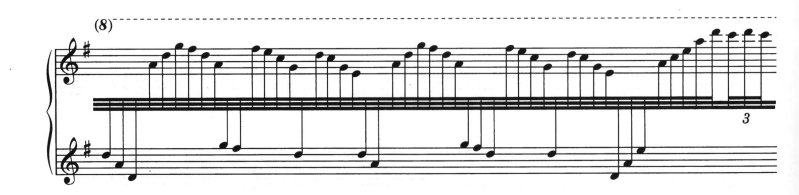

Tempo I° (liberamente)

poco più mosso   **a tempo**   **rit.**

a tempo

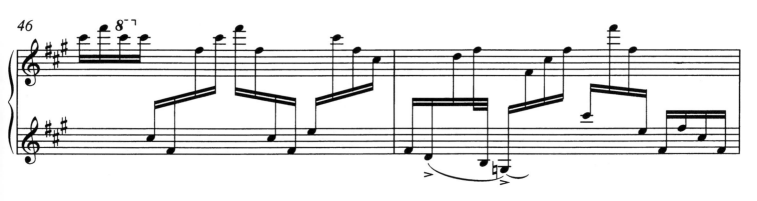

poco a poco cresc.

The Art of Flying

6 August

Sztuka latania

Zbigniew Preisner
Interpreted by Leszek Możdżer

*Back home again, returning to life, same turmoil, phones, faxes? …
just true life. Or the art of flying.*

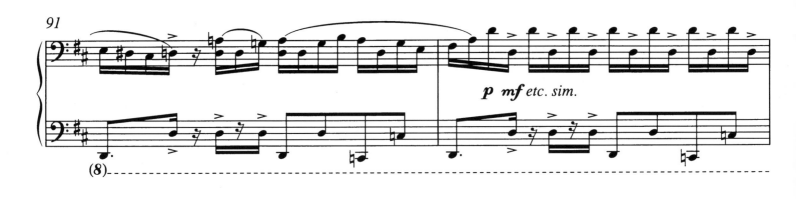

About Passing

O przemijaniu

1 November

Zbigniew Preisner
Interpreted by Leszek Możdżer

The list of those absent is a long one. Those who have passed away forever and those whom you cannot see any more, though they live as if across the street. Such losses are painful.

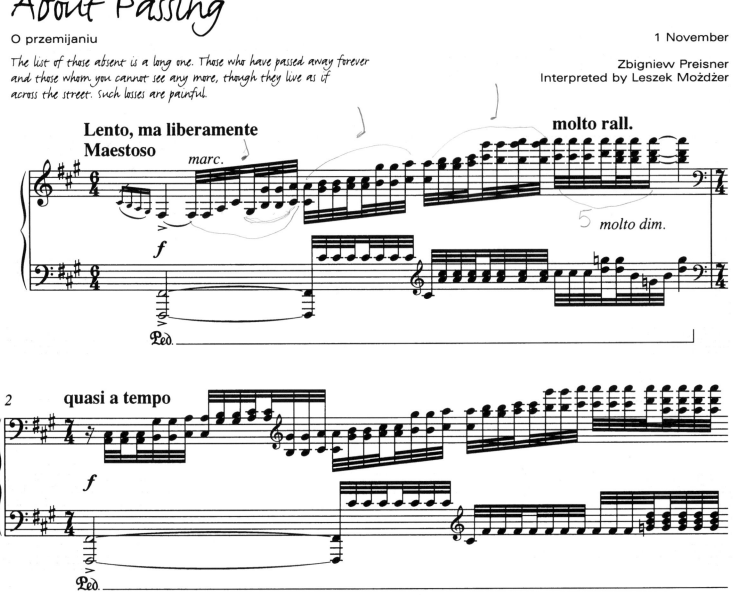

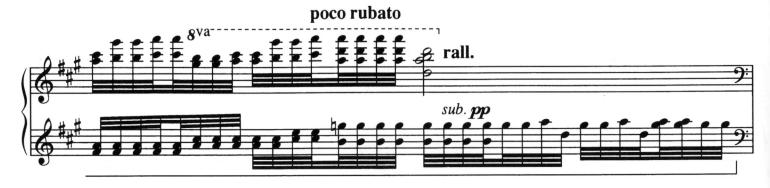

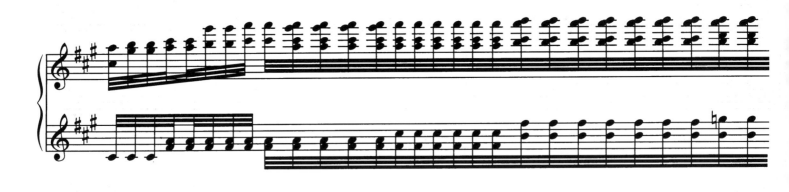

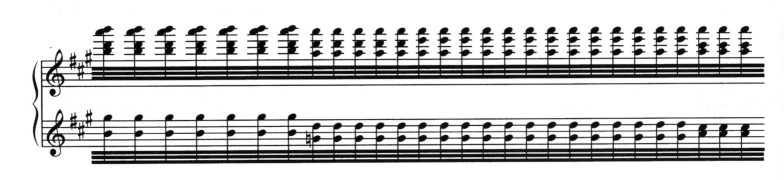

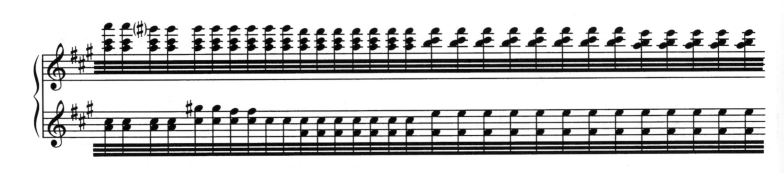

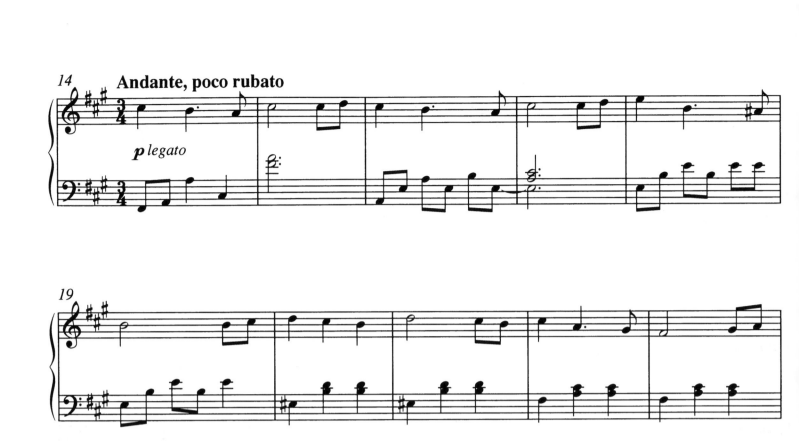

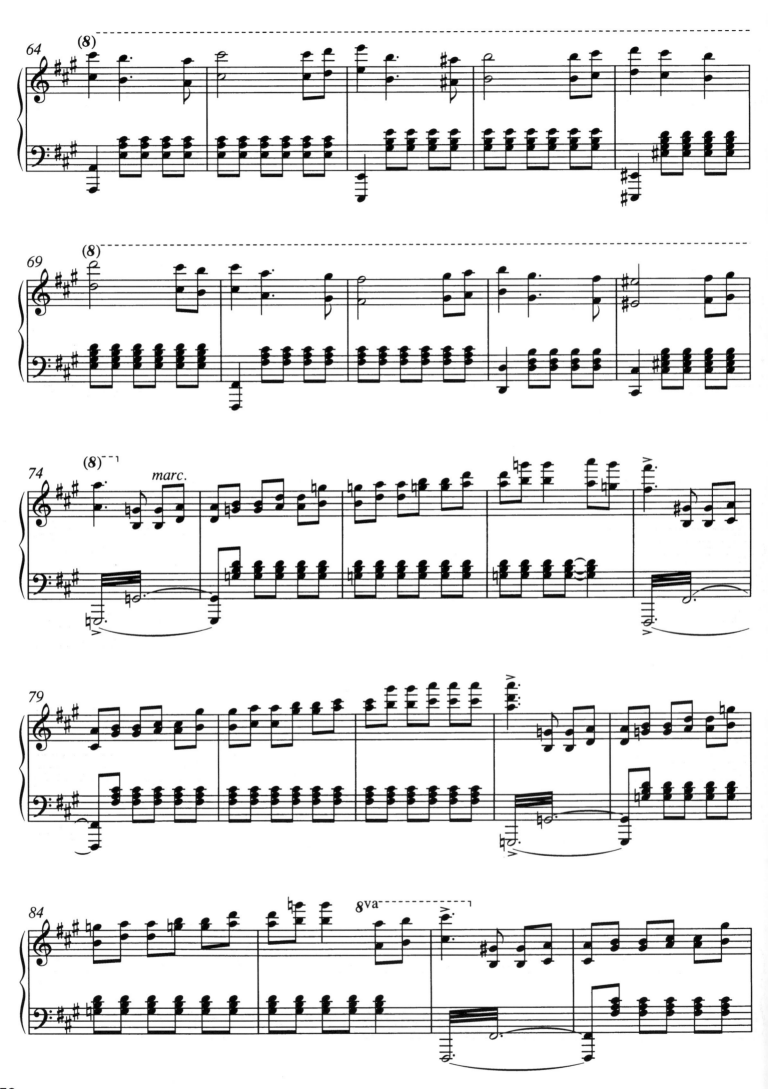

Farewell

Pożegnanie

I don't like:
finishing a song
completing work on a new film
finishing any structure, no matter how unreasonable it is
ending another project in my life
bidding farewell to people; and that is what I hate most.

11 November

Zbigniew Preisner
Interpreted by Leszek Możdżer

poco a poco cresc.

mf

A Tune a Day

Już gram

I am already grasping things, just walking, just speaking,
just thinking, just playing, I just know that I know nothing.

1 December

Zbigniew Preisner
Interpreted by Leszek Możdżer

rall.

Greetings from Pamalican

Pamalican, the Philippines. 26 February 1999

Zbigniew Preisner
Interpreted by Leszek Możdżer

Pozdrowienia z Pamalican

Paradise on Earth begins somewhere here, at the depth of seven metres and extends some 40 metres underwater. Below is only the 'deep blue'. It involves you, very much so.

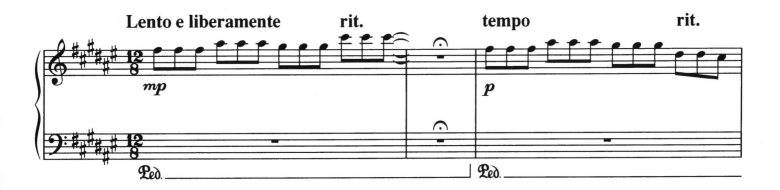

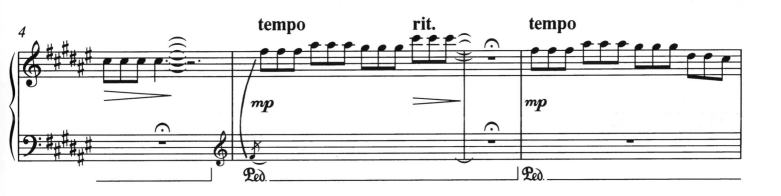

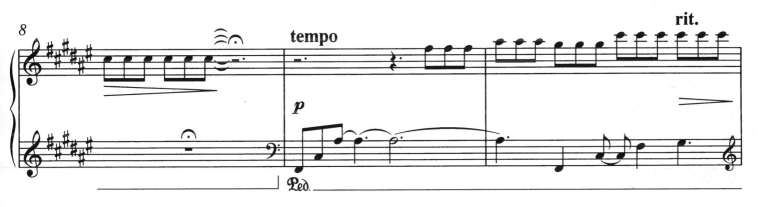

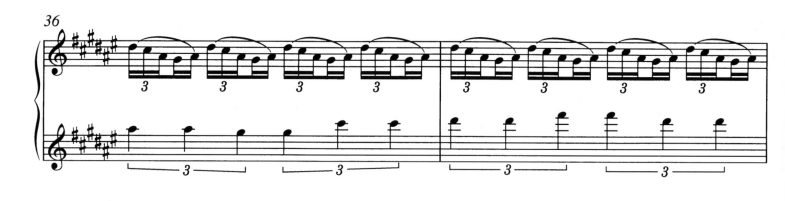

senza misura
(molto irregolare)

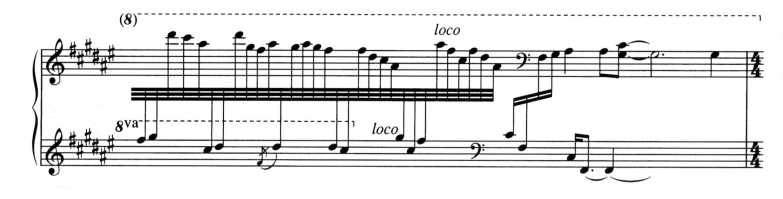

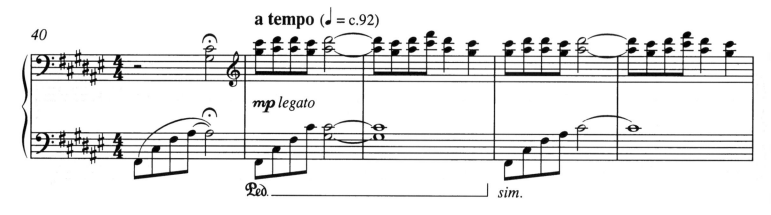

A Good Night Melody

Melodia na dobranoc

1 April

I'm falling asleep and will be dreaming again, or maybe somebody calls in to talk, or i'll visit someone. Or, maybe, we will all meet at the same place. Every night may be the last night.

Zbigniew Preisner
Interpreted by Leszek Możdżer

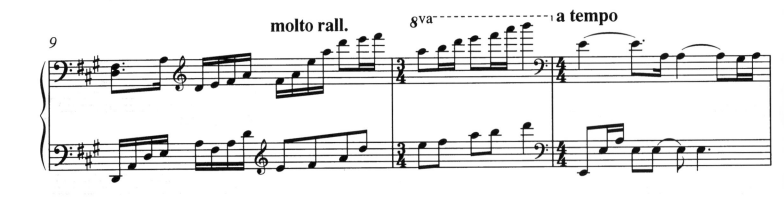

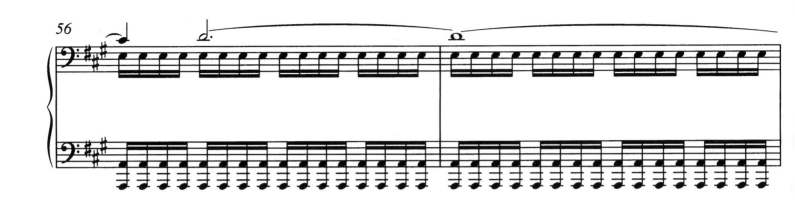

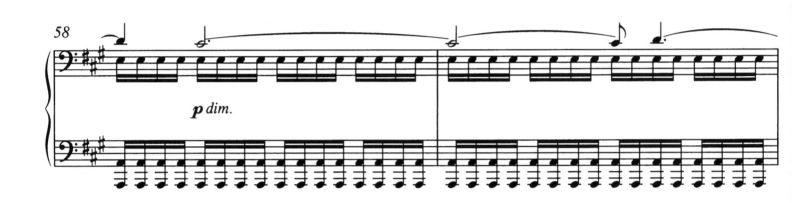

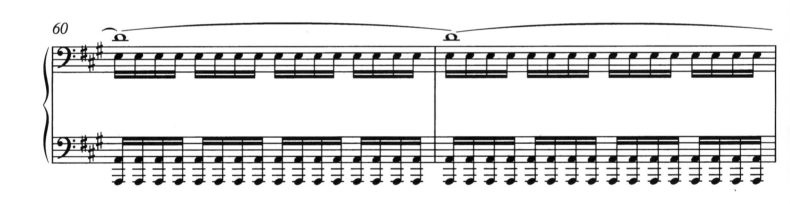

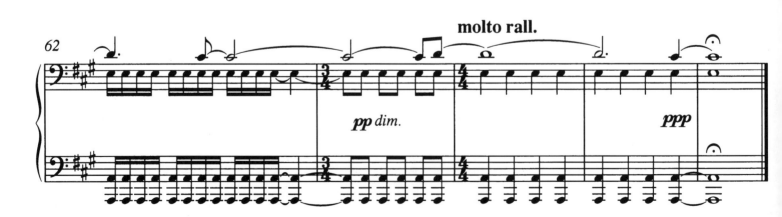